HUMMINGBIRDS

of the American West

LYNN HASSLER KAUFMAN

Rio Nuevo Publishers
Tucson, Arizona

Cover: Female broad-tailed hummingbird

Title page: Female black-chinned hummingbird extends tongue to capture insect on prickly pear flower.

Rio Nuevo Publishers
An imprint of Treasure Chest Books
P.O. Box 5250
Tucson, AZ 85703-0250

Editor: Ronald J. Foreman
Designer: William Benoit, Simpson & Convent

Photographs
© David Bertelsen: 59, 71
© Rick & Nora Bowers: 21, 23, 33, 34, 35
© Russell C. Hansen: Front cover, 4, 9, 28, 29, 30, 31, 41
© Lynn Hassler Kaufman: 58, 60, 62, 63, 66-67, 68, 70
© Anthony Marcieca: 7, 17, 27, 52
© Charles W. Melton: 11, 19, 20, 24, 25, 26, 36, 37, 38, 39, 42, 44, 46, 47, 48, 49, 51, 64, 65, 69
© C. Allan Morgan: iv, 10, 12, 40, 61
© Brian E. Small: 45
© Tom Vezo: Title page, 14, 18, 43, 50, 55, 74

Front cover: Female broad-tailed hummingbird, Russell C. Hansen
Title page: Female black-chinned hummingbird, Tom Vezo

Library of Congress Cataloging-in-Publication Data

Kaufman, Lynn Hassler.
    Hummingbirds of the American West / Lynn Hassler Kaufman
        p. cm.
    ISBN 1-887896-27-9
1.   Hummingbirds—West (U.S.) I. Title.

QL69'64'0978—dc21   2001005236

Printed in Korea
10   9   8   7   6   5   4   3   2   1

TABLE OF CONTENTS

Male Costa's hummingbird hovers at Penstemon *ssp.*

INTRODUCTION

Hummingbirds are, in a word, mesmerizing. With wings buzzing and a-blur, these diminutive creatures seem to defy the laws of physics and flight. Hummers are remarkably agile: they can hover in one spot and have a unique ability to fly up, down, sideways, and even backwards. Their wings beat so rapidly that we often *hear* their unmistakable humming before we see them, and as they zig and zag through the air they appear to be everywhere at once. Certainly, no other birds exhibit such focused, frenetic activity, flitting from flower to flower and probing each colorful reservoir for life-giving nectar.

Males are the real showmen of this group, graced with iridescent crowns and throats that make them look like tiny gemstones come to life. Few other birds exhibit so many sparkling colors. In South America, where hummingbirds most likely originated and where they are most numerous, some hummingbirds carry visually evocative names such as sapphire, emerald, brilliant, coquette, and sunangel.

Hummingbirds are members of the order Apodiformes that also includes birds called swifts, which also are known for their distinctively tapered wings and agility in flight. The apodi- prefix literally means "without feet." Hummingbirds and swifts do have feet, of course, but their legs are very short and they are unable to walk or hop.

Within the order Apodiformes, hummingbirds belong to a group called Trochilidae, which is unique to the western hemisphere. They are found in a variety of habitats and elevations from coastal regions to deserts to high mountain ranges of 10,000 feet or higher. Estimates as to the number of hummingbird species hover around three hundred twenty, and the closer one gets to the equator the more species one is apt to find. More species live in Ecuador and Colombia than anywhere else. The smallest bird on earth—a mere 2¼ inches long—is the bee hummingbird of Cuba. The largest hummingbird—at 8½ inches—is the giant hummingbird of the South American Andes.

Not surprisingly, hummingbirds held extraordinary spiritual significance for the ancient Aztecs of Mesoamerica. They believed that their bravest warriors who died in battle would be reincarnated as hummingbirds, and they also used the bright, colorful feathers of these birds to decorate clothing worn by priests and royalty. Huitzilopochtli, the Aztec god of the hunt, was even depicted wearing a helmet resembling a hummingbird's head.

In the United States, the greatest number of hummingbird species occurs in the West, and in particular the subtropical Southwest, where the region's wide range of elevations supports a greater diversity of plants and habitats. At least fifteen different species spend all or part of each year in the deserts and mountains of southeastern Arizona. Although most of our hummingbirds travel south into Mexico after the nesting season, small numbers migrate east in the fall, and a surprising number of species can be found scattered through the southeastern U.S. in winter. However, only one species—the ruby-throated hummingbird—is commonly found east of the Mississippi River.

This book covers eighteen hummingbird species found in the western United States and Canada, as well as three accidentals—species that are rarely seen north of Mexico. For the purposes of this book, the American West is defined as that large expanse from the Pacific Coast to the Great Plains. Species accounts are arranged in taxonomic order, which means they are placed in the sequence of their presumed natural relationships. The sequence for this book is based on the classification approved by the American Ornithologists' Union current at the time of publication.

This book also contains a section on gardening for humming-birds with a recommended list of native plants that will attract them. With their almost constant activity and motion, humming-birds will enliven any garden and provide endless hours of enjoyment and entertainment. And as you learn more about these tiny birds, marvels of the avian world, I hope you will become more motivated to connect with the mysteries and adventures of the natural world, and more committed to preserving it.

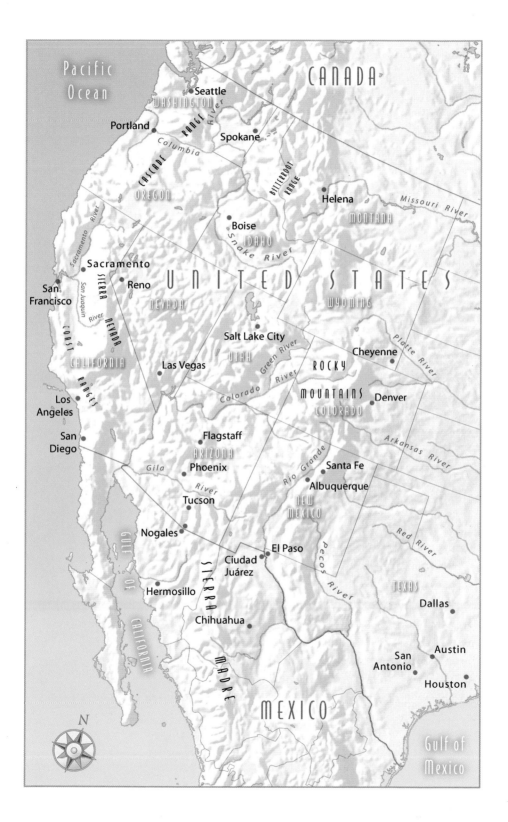

Pacific
Ocean

CANADA

Seattle
WASHINGTON
Portland
Spokane
Columbia River
CASCADE RANGE
OREGON
BITTERROOT RANGE
Helena
MONTANA
Missouri River
Boise
IDAHO
Snake River
Sacramento
SIERRA
Reno
UNITED STATES
San
Francisco
San Juaquin River
Sacramento River
NEVADA
NEVADA
WYOMING
COAST
Salt Lake City
UTAH
Green River
Cheyenne
Platte River
CALIFORNIA
RANGES
Las Vegas
Colorado River
ROCKY
MOUNTAINS
Denver
COLORADO
Los
Angeles
San
Diego
Flagstaff
ARIZONA
Phoenix
Gila River
Rio Grande
Santa Fe
Albuquerque
NEW
MEXICO
Arkansas River
Tucson
Nogales
El Paso
Pecos River
Red River
Ciudad
Juárez
GULF
Hermosillo
SIERRA
TEXAS
Dallas
OF
Chihuahua
MADRE
San
Antonio
Austin
CALIFORNIA
Houston
MEXICO
N
Gulf of
Mexico

Male blue-throated hummingbird keeps wings stiff in flight.

PHYSICAL CHARACTERISTICS

Flight

Hummingbirds are remarkable in many ways. First and foremost, they have the fastest wingbeat rates of any bird. Wingbeats may exceed seventy-two times per second—a speed difficult for us to even imagine. Hummingbirds can also control their positions in the air like no other bird and change direction on a dime. One of the most remarkable aspects of their flight is their ability to hover, giving them a distinct advantage for feeding at many kinds of flowers.

What physiological characteristics enable hummingbirds to fly with such maneuverability and speed? Their flight muscles account for 25-30 percent of total body weight, which can range from 2 to 8 grams, depending on the species. This is relatively large in proportion to other flying birds, whose flight muscles typically represent only 15-25 percent of their body weight. Hummingbirds also have special adaptations for hovering. Most birds bend their wings at joints that are similar to the shoulder, elbow, and wrist in humans, but hummingbirds tend to keep their wings very stiff in flight, rotating them mainly at the shoulder. As they hover, their wings move forward and backward. Wings also swivel to achieve lift on both the forward and backward strokes, in much the same way as we move our arms when we tread water.

Metabolism

Hummers have the most rapid heartbeat of any bird; at rest, their hearts beat about eight times faster than the average human heart. Their metabolic rate—the rate at which food is converted to heat and energy—is the fastest of any animal. Their tiny bodies dissipate excess heat rapidly, and they have little capacity for storing energy in the form of fat. Thus, during waking hours, they are focused on feeding.

Because they burn up their fuel so quickly, hummingbirds are at a disadvantage if nighttime temperatures dip below a certain level. Nature has a remarkable solution for this problem: a special resting or dormant state, called torpor, in which body temperatures and energy requirements both drop. Heartbeats slow and breathing may become irregular. Food stored in the crop, at the base of the bird's throat, helps sustain them overnight. Hummingbirds do not enter torpor every night; it is undoubtedly a contingency measure when energy reserves are low. Determining factors include climatic conditions, diet, and seasonal behavior variations. Hummingbirds are able to stay in this resting state for about eight hours. When their body temperatures warm up to about 86 degrees, they are able to fly again.

Feeding

Each day, the average hummer must consume about half its weight in food. Flower nectar is the primary food source but, in the absence of blooms, hummingbirds may eat large quantities of tiny insects and spiders. Gnats, flies, mosquitoes, aphids, and flying ants all serve as a source of protein. Some larger species of hummingbirds have proportionately lower energy requirements than smaller species and tend to eat more insects. As a substitute for flower nectar, some of the more northerly hummingbirds may feed on oozing tree sap from holes produced by sapsuckers.

Not all feeding at flowers or feeders is done while hovering; if convenient, birds may perch on a twig or stem. Feeding is characterized by several pauses in which the hummer may remove its bill from the flower. Hummingbirds locate food by sight and, like most other birds, have a poorly developed sense of smell. Their tongues are flat, with grooves or troughs on the edges that aid in gathering insects and nectar, and they are sometimes barbed.

For the most part, hummingbird territories are determined by the amount of food available. In nature, flowers do not continually produce nectar, and cannot immediately replace nectar that has been removed. The process of regenerating nectar takes time. In response, some species of hummingbirds use a strategy called traplining, in which they go from plant to plant on a regular circuit, avoiding flowers they have visited recently to enable them to regenerate the nectar pool.

Despite how it may seem, hummingbirds do not feed continually. They must spend some time digesting. They generally feed about 5-8 times per hour. If you notice a hummingbird sitting quietly on a branch or perch, it probably is transferring stored nectar or insects from its crop into the active part of its digestive tract. When the crop is about half empty, the bird will fly off again to gather more food.

Female white-eared hummingbird at Castilleja *ssp.*

Territoriality

Observers are often amazed at the aggressive nature of humming-birds and the way they chase away other birds. The birds are simply being territorial; that is, defending flowers or food sources within a certain area. This behavior probably evolved because sources of nectar in nature are limited. A bird instinctively knows that it takes less energy, and is thus more efficient, to defend existing, good sources of nectar from other hummingbirds than to seek out new flowers. Hummingbirds may also chase away butterflies, bees, and other pollinators. This behavior is so deeply ingrained that it carries over to sugar water feeders. They continue to defend "their" food source, even though there may be a nearly endless supply of sweet water provided by the backyard birdwatcher.

Life span

Most hummingbirds do not live longer than about three to five years. Mortality is high, particularly among young birds. However, there are records of banded individuals living to the ripe old age of twelve. Weather often plays a significant role in mortality. Extreme drought or cold conditions can drastically reduce the availability of nectar and insects. In North America, there is no one predator that specializes on hummingbirds, but there are several that will take them on occasion. Natural predators include other birds such as roadrunners, large flycatchers, and small, agile raptors such as sharp-shinned hawks. Even large praying mantises have been seen capturing hummingbirds. Some hummers get caught and trapped in spider webs. Others reach an untimely demise by accidentally flying into cars or windows.

BEHAVIOR

Vocalizations

Hummingbirds have many amazing attributes, but melodious song is not one of them. Their vocalizations tend to be squeaks, whistles, chirps, cheeps, ticks, clacks, hums, and buzzes—hardly musical in the traditional sense. Green violet-ear and Anna's hummingbird vocalize much of the time, and the latter's chatter is particularly distinctive.

Many of the sounds hummingbirds make are non-vocal. This group of birds is aptly named for the unique sound they make in flight—a hum that is sometimes confused with the sound of an insect. Hummingbirds make many specialized sounds as they fly or dive through the air. An example of a distinctive wing sound is the high-pitched trilling made by certain feathers of the broad-tailed hummingbird in flight.

Female broad-tailed hummingbird

Courtship and nesting

Adult hummingbirds tend to live a solitary existence and seek out other adults only for the purpose of mating. Most male hummingbirds are promiscuous, mating with multiple females each season.

Males perform elaborate, stylized courtship displays, many of which are described in the species accounts in this book. Each species conducts its own individualized, spellbinding show, performing distinctive flight patterns to get the attention of the females, and perhaps to warn other males to stay away. During

Mother broad-tailed hummingbird arrives to feed young.

these displays, a male typically spreads the feathers of his gorget, or throat patch, and then whizzes through the air to impress the female with his stunning colors and aerial acrobatics. The act of copulation is brief—a few seconds at most—and no pair bond is formed.

Female hummingbirds do all the nest building, incubation, and tending of the young. Females may return to established nest sites, but rarely use the same nest without completely or at least partially reconstructing it. They collect plant fibers, lichens, pieces of bark, and other bits of plant material to form their small, cuplike nests. Frequently, they use spider webbing to bind the nesting materials together, and line the nest with downy plant material and other soft plant parts. Hummingbird nests are elastic, able to stretch to accommodate the growing young.

Female hummingbirds lay the smallest eggs of any bird. Eggs are about the size of lima beans, and the female generally lays two, about a day apart. The incubation period may be anywhere from 2-2½ weeks, depending on the species. The baby birds are born blind, and without feathers.

Baby hummingbirds are born blind, without feathers.

To watch the female feed her young is quite a spectacle. Young birds open their mouths in response to the wing action of the adult female as she flies in to feed them nectar and insects, which she has stored in her crop. She sticks her bill directly down the throat of each nestling, regurgitating food directly into the young bird's crop. The young look as if they are being impaled, rather than receiving life-giving nutrients.

Of course, amid all of this frantic activity—building the nest, laying and incubating the eggs, feeding the young—the female also must find time to feed herself.

Young birds are generally nest-bound for about twenty days. As they get close to leaving the nest, they begin standing on the edge to exercise their wings and legs. Finally they are ready to depart to begin their own frenzied lifestyles. They continue to grow even after leaving the nest.

Bathing and preening

Preening is a basic function that birds perform to care for their feathers. A bird preens by grasping the base of a feather with its bill and nibbling along the feather toward the tip to remove oil, dirt, and parasites. Birds may also draw a single feather through their partly clamped bills in one movement to smooth the feather barbs and remove dirt. During preening, the hummingbird often fluffs out its body feathers in order to reach them more easily, bending and twisting its neck and head to reach more inaccessible places. They may also rub their bills on twigs or branches. Preening often follows bathing.

Male black-chinned hummingbird drinking.

Although hummingbirds do most of their drinking while sipping nectar from flowers, they regularly seek out water, both for drinking and bathing. They tend to prefer running water and may take baths on the wing while hovering under the spray from a hose or sprinkler. They also may use beads of water on vegetation, fluttering their wings among leaves that are covered with accumulations of dew. For hummingbirds to use birdbaths, they must be very shallow. Using rocks to create different depths is often helpful.

Migration

Most hummingbirds in the tropics are non-migratory or short distance migrants, but all of ours migrate to some degree. Rufous hummingbird is a long distance champion, flying nearly three thousand miles from its wintering grounds in central Mexico to its breeding grounds in southern Alaska. Ruby-throated hummingbirds may fly five hundred miles nonstop across the Gulf of Mexico and beyond during migration. Energized by stored fat, they increase their body weight by some 50 percent in order to fuel the long haul. During migratory flight, their wings may beat at about sixty times per second, and birds can reach speeds of 25 mph. The fact that these diminutive creatures are able to survive such long, heroic journeys is one of life's small miracles.

The urge to migrate is triggered by changing day length and seems to be timed to the blooming seasons of flowers. Birds are also able to sense weather fronts that may be favorable for migration. Depending on the species, migration may take several months. Hummingbirds migrate as individuals, not in flocks like geese or ducks, so they seem to be guided by an internal compass. Adults may be able to remember certain landmarks along the way, but young hummingbirds making their first migration alone must rely on other cues, with no help from their elders.

LOOKING AT HUMMINGBIRDS

Plumage and identification

Males are more brilliantly colored in most hummingbird species. Their brilliant, iridescent throat patches, or gorgets, vary in size, depending upon the species. In some species, the gorget is very small, while in others it may extend down the chest and around both sides of the neck. Seeing color on the gorget can be tricky. Often, the throat just looks dark or black. It is only when the light hits it in just the right way that one can perceive color.

*Male broad-tailed hummingbird. Feather structures,
rather than pigment, create iridescent colors.*

Females and young birds tend to be much duller and can be challenging to identify. Young birds, regardless of sex, look fairly similar to adult females at first. Most lack the gorget and most have white spots on the tail feathers

Even experts may experience difficulty making a positive identification. For example, distinguishing between the female and young rufous and Allen's can only be reliably done if birds are netted and held in the hand. If you're just starting out to identify hummingbirds, try focusing on the males until you get a feel for shape, size, and behavior.

Iridescence

Many of the colorful hues seen on hummingbirds are created by the structure of their feathers rather than by actual pigment. The distinctive coloration is created by the reflection of light off filmy layers on the birds' feathers. As light hits these layers, it is reflected or broken down by refraction into iridescent colors.

The feather structure of a male hummingbird's crown and throat directs reflected light in a single direction, and produces the effect of magically changing colors as the bird flies about— from color to dark or black. Conversely, the structure of the feathers on the back diffuses the reflection of light, scattering it in multiple directions and giving the appearance of a single color—usually green—no matter what the viewing angle.

Hummingbird look-alikes

If you see a small creature hovering at flowers, especially around dusk, it might be a sphinx or hawk moth rather than a humming-bird. Sphinx moths feed on nectar, often from tubular-shaped flowers, and pollinate them in the same manner as hummingbirds. They also hover at flowers while they sip nectar with their long tongues. Most species are out at night or dusk, but some kinds are seen in broad daylight. The name sphinx moth comes from the caterpillars, which are able to pull their bodies into sphinxlike poses.

Green Violet-ear

Colibri thalassinus

Spanish
Chupaflor orejivioleta verde

Range: Highlands of Mexico south to Bolivia; one or two wander into south or central Texas almost every year, and the species has strayed as far east as North Carolina and as far north as Canada.

Few other hummingbirds are as wide-ranging as the nomadic green violet-ear. Unlike most tropical hummingbirds, which are more localized, this species can be found in the mountains from Mexico all the way to Bolivia in South America. Within this broad range, it is fairly nomadic and numbers of individuals are continually on the move. Given its wide distribution, it is not surprising that green violet-ear has been found straying into North America.

These are glittering green, elegant-looking humming-birds. The bird is named for its violet "ear," a patch of purple feathers that extends from below the eye to the nape. When agitated, birds often fan these sparkling purple feathers. A patch of violet-blue also shows on the breast. Females are similar, but duller in color with a very small or absent breast patch. Tails of both sexes are mostly blue with a black band near the tip.

Males of this species do not seem to participate in stylized courtship displays. Instead they form loose groups, perch high in trees, and sing endlessly. Their song, characterized by some as one of the most monotonous songs of the tropics, is an unchanging series of dry notes. Females build deep, bulky nests using small leaves, mosses, grass blades, and spider webbing. As with most hummers, they lay two white eggs.

Broad-billed Hummingbird

Cynanthus latirostris

Spanish
Chupaflor piquiancho

Range: March to September in limited areas of Arizona and extreme southwest New Mexico; winters mainly in Mexico, but small numbers may winter in southern Arizona.

♀

One of the most colorful hummingbirds in North America, the male broad-bill is reminiscent of a sparkling jewel with its dark green body and glistening blue gorget. Its bright red-orange bill is tipped with black. Males have forked tails that are completely bluish black in color. The tails of females also show a lot of blue-black, but the outer tail feathers are pale tipped. Females also have grayish underparts and light eye stripes. Bills are reddish orange at the base. The broad-bill's voice is a distinctive series of dry, crackling notes, and both males and females make a loud chattering call when alarmed.

Broad-billed hummingbirds have a limited U.S. range, but are quite abundant where they are found—in riparian zones of arid canyons in southeast Arizona and very locally in southwest New Mexico. Destruction of riparian habitat is a cause of concern for the future status of this species.

For his courtship ritual, the male makes a pendulum-like display, a side-to-side arc performed directly in front of the female. He makes several sweeps back and forth, and then a couple of vertical passes. Following this exhibition, he may fly to a nearby perch. He may also fly in the direction of the target female, whereupon a fast and furious chase ensues. The faster beat of his wings is actually audible during this mating display.

Broad-bills nest in deciduous shrubs, vines, or the low branches of trees, generally three to nine feet above the ground. Females use their long, needlelike bills to weave material into cup-shaped nests. Unlike most other North American hummingbirds, they do not use lichen on the outside of nest. Nest predation by snakes may be a problem because the nests are usually so low to the ground.

Flowers the broad-bill feasts upon include those of agaves, desert honeysuckle, bouvardia, paintbrush, coral bean, penstemon, ocotillo, and betony.

♂

White-eared Hummingbird

Hylocharis leucotis

Spanish
Chupaflor oreji-blanco

Range: Mexican border to Nicaragua; a few reach the southwestern U.S.

This bird is very abundant in Mexico's Sierra Madre, but a few individuals reach canyons in southeast Arizona nearly every year. In Arizona, they are generally found in mountain canyons where hummingbird feeders are maintained. Occasionally, an individual will over-winter at a feeder.

Male white-eared hummingbirds sport a bright red bill tipped with black, a blackish blue tail, and a long white stripe behind the eye (hence the name). Their throats reflect blue and green, and their crowns are purple. Female birds also show the long white stripe behind the eye. They may resemble female broad-billed hummingbirds but have shorter bills, less blue black on the tails, and their underparts are whitish with numerous green spots.

♂

♀

For their call note, white-eared hummingbirds make a hard, metallic clicking sound.

White-eared hummingbirds are quite distinctive in their courtship habits. Males gather in loose groups, perch between sixty and one hundred feet apart, and sing short songs to attract females. The usual nest site is five to twenty feet above ground on a twig or in the fork of a shrub or tree.

Berylline Hummingbird
Amazilia beryllina

Spanish
Amazilia Alicastaña

Range: Western and southern Mexico, Guatemala, Honduras, El Salvador; a few reach southeastern Arizona every summer.

Since 1964, this hummingbird has been a rare but regular visitor to the U.S. When it does show up north of the Mexican border, it tends to remain in the area for months at a time. Berylline hummingbirds have nested in southern Arizona several times.

Named for the color of beryl, a naturally occurring metal that is typically turquoise or blue-green, berylline hummingbirds have glittering apple-green heads and bodies with reddish brown wings, rump, and tail. Males and females look similar, although the females tend to be duller with gray bellies. Bill color is mostly black with a touch of red. The three-noted song of the berylline hummingbird sounds like a tiny trumpet, with the last note being noticeably higher in pitch.

These birds are not particularly conspicuous. When perched, they are often overlooked because they do not call attention to themselves. Over most of their range, they inhabit foothills and the lower slopes of mountains, especially in areas of oak woodland. In Arizona, they prefer shady canyons among sycamores or open pine-oak woodlands between 5,000-7,000 feet elevation. Berylline hummingbirds usually nest between seventeen and thirty-five feet above the ground on a horizontal branch. When in Arizona, they usually select a sycamore tree for their nesting site.

Buff-bellied Hummingbird

Amazilia yucatanensis

Spanish
Colibrí Yucateco

Range: Resident in Mexico, Belize, and Guatemala; mostly summer resident in south Texas.

Part of the tropical element in south Texas, buff-bellied hummingbirds are often seen visiting flowers such as red salvia, Turk's cap, coral bean, and shrimp plant. This species is not as particular as some hummingbirds about feeding on tubular-shaped flowers, and will visit a wide variety of blossoms of all colors and shapes.

Relatively common in southern Texas in summer, some individuals remain through the winter. A few move north along the gulf coast in fall, and winter on the upper Texas coast and in Louisiana—an unusual northerly movement for hummingbirds. Some individuals occasionally over-winter even farther east. Not particularly fussy about habitat, buff-bellied hummingbirds can be found in open woodlands, clearings, and suburban gardens.

These are medium-sized hummingbirds with bronzy green backs and chestnut tails. The throat and upper breast are a shiny metallic emerald green, and the lower breast and belly a cinnamon buff.

♂

♀

Unlike most North American species, the sexes are similar in appearance. Their bills are pinkish red with a black tip. Their call note is a metallic scraping sound.

Buff-bellied hummingbirds usually nest in large shrubs or small deciduous trees such as hackberry, Texas ebony, or cordia. Nests are relatively low to the ground, about three to ten feet high on a horizontal or drooping branch or in the horizontal fork of a twig. Females often refurbish or build on the top of old nests. They generally lay two eggs, and probably produce only one brood per season.

The species name *yucatanensis* literally means "from the Yucatan," a reference to part of the bird's native range.

Violet-crowned Hummingbird

Amazilia violiceps

Spanish

Chupamirto corona azul

Range: Mainly western Mexico, regular in summer in a few places in southeast Arizona and southwest New Mexico.

A recent arrival to the U.S., violet-crowned hummingbird was virtually unknown north of the Mexican border until the late 1950s, and it is still quite scarce and localized. Violet-crowned hummingbirds frequent arid or semiarid open woodlands. When found in the U.S., they are usually near groves of tall trees, especially sycamores and cottonwoods, surrounded by a brushy understory.

During the breeding season, violet-crowned hummingbirds deliver a squeaky song that often can be heard at dawn. For their nesting sites they favor deciduous trees, especially sycamores, or large shrubs. Nests are placed in open but shady spots four to forty feet from the ground.

On the large size for hummers, this species is about four and one half inches long. The sexes look similar with bright white underparts and throats, bronzy green upperparts, and green tails. The bill is bright red and tipped with black. Crown color is a violet-blue, and is slightly duller in the female.

♂

♀

When flower nectar is not abundant or available, violet-crowned hummingbirds can be seen hovering mid-level in the shade of tall trees, catching insects. The species name *violiceps* is from the Greek meaning "violethead," a reference to the bird's violet-blue crown.

Blue-throated Hummingbird

Lampornis clemenciae

Spanish

Chupamirto garganta azul, Chupaflor gorgiazul

Range: Southwestern U.S. to southern Mexico.

About the size of some sparrows, blue-throated hummingbirds are the largest of the U.S. breeding hummingbirds. They are over five inches long and weigh more than three times as much as the medium-sized ruby-throated hummingbird. Because of their large size and longer wings, they fly with fewer wing-beats per second than the smaller hummers.

Blue-throated hummingbirds are green above and have conspicuous facial markings—two white facial stripes—and a large black tail with white corners. Males have dark throats with blue iridescence, which is often difficult to see, and gray underparts. The throats of the females are gray.

As might be expected from their large size, blue-throats have a highly combative nature. Approaching other hummingbirds at flowers or feeders, they aggressively spread their tail feathers, showing the flashy black and white pattern, and then chase away the interlopers. This tail fanning display is particularly

♀

♂

noticeable in flight. Males have a loud, squeaky *seek* call note, often delivered in flight.

Blue-throats favor shady spots near water, and can generally be found along wooded streams in lower mountain canyons. They often nest streamside on a branch sheltered by an overhanging limb, under the eaves of buildings, or under bridges. The outer covering of their nest is green moss, unique among North American hummer nests.

Relatively flexible in their choice of flowers, blue-throated hummingbirds will feed at blossoms of various shapes and colors. They also eat large numbers of insects and spiders, probably more than most U.S. hummingbird species.

In Greek, the genus name *Lampornis* translates to "lampbird."

Magnificent Hummingbird

Eugenes fulgens

Spanish
Chupaflor magnifico

Range: Southwestern U.S. to Panama; strays have been seen as far north as Minnesota.

Formerly called Rivoli's hummingbird, after the Duke of Rivoli, this bird's name was changed in the early 1980s to magnificent hummingbird. The species name *fulgens* is from the Latin *fulgere*, meaning to gleam or glitter.

At a distance, this very large hummingbird looks all dark. Males have nearly black bellies, which is unique among North American hummers, bright emerald-green throats, and purple crowns. Females are green above and dusky green below with spotted throats and subtle pale corners to the tail. Head size is relatively large compared to body size in this species, and the birds have rather flat-looking foreheads. About five inches long, magnificent hummingbird is the second largest hummer in North America. As with the large blue-throat, the slower wingbeats of these birds are nearly discernible in flight.

Their large size enables the male birds to enter into the territories of smaller species and remain relatively unmolested. They are also

♀

♂

very efficient in driving off intruders who happen to enter their own territories. Adult males make a *chip* note while perched or in flight, and when alarmed, deliver an aggressive chatter of notes.

In North America, the breeding range of this species is limited to mountain ranges of southern Arizona, New Mexico, and west Texas. These are birds of pine-oak woodlands interspersed with sycamore and coniferous trees. Nests are typically ten to sixty feet above ground on a horizontal branch in the open area of a tree such as pine or maple. Magnificent hummingbirds typically leave the U.S. in late September or early October following the nesting season, although one will occasionally linger at a feeder over the winter months.

Magnificent hummingbirds visit the flowers of agave, red columbine (*Aquilegia triternata*), paintbrush (*Castilleja* spp.), bouvardia (*Bouvardia ternifolia*), beardtongue (*Penstemon barbatus*), and some sages (*Salvia lemmoni*). There is some speculation that this species may consume more insects than nectar.

Plain-capped Starthroat

Heliomaster constantii

Spanish
Heliomáster flanquigrís

Range: Mexico and Central America; rare wanderer into southern Arizona.

This large, rather drab hummingbird is a rare visitor to southern Arizona in the summer and fall months. It also has wandered as far north as the suburbs of Phoenix. It tends to favor riparian habitat with tall trees at middle elevations in mountain canyons. In its native range in Mexico, the plain-capped starthroat is found in dry thorn forests and river edges where it is often seen hovering over rivers or roads, catching insects.

The sexes of this species look similar. Males and females have red throats, but the color is often difficult to see, and the red on the female is more restricted and sometimes totally lacking. The color on the throat is bordered by a conspicuous white whisker stripe and white behind the eye. Plain-capped starthroats have dull crowns and white tufts near the base of the wings. They also have a distinctive patch of white on the rump. Their voice is a sharp *chip* or *cheep*.

The name of the genus *Heliomaster* means "sun-loving."

Lucifer Hummingbird

Calothorax lucifer

♂

Spanish
Colibrí Lucifer

Range: West Texas to southern Mexico; locally in summer in southeast Arizona and southwest New Mexico.

L ucifer hummingbird inhabits arid, open, and often rugged habitats where it frequents flowering ocotillo and agave stalks. Mainly birds of central and northern Mexico, a few reach the southwestern U.S. each year. Males have dazzling purple throats and sides of the neck, buff-colored sides, and a long forked tail that usually is tightly folded. Females have a buff-colored breast and a pale streak behind the eye. The long, downward-curving bill of this species is distinctive, although length and curvature of the bill can vary greatly.

The male has a unique courtship display. which he performs in front of the female at her nest. He makes multiple short flights back and forth, and in so doing produces loud, rustling sounds with his wings. He then flies high and dives steeply past the nest. Lucifer males are unusual in that they display at the nest site. In most other species of hummingbirds, the location of the nest has no apparent connection to the display ritual. The female Lucifer's nest is generally found in open cholla cactus, on ocotillo stems, or agave stalks, two to ten feet from the ground.

Lucifer hummingbirds are particularly attracted to the flowers of agave plants. The larger species of agave are adapted for pollination by bats and generally produce more nectar than hummingbird-adapted flowers. The Lucifer takes advantage of this by feeding during the day-time on any surplus nectar left in the agave flower. Since the flowers of the agave are designed differently from the classic hummingbird flower, the Lucifer acts as a non-pollinating nectar thief because it makes no contact with the sexual parts of the plant. Dead agave flower stalks often attract other competing nectar feeders such as carpenter bees, which use the dead stalks as nesting sites. When bees are present, they may cut out the bases of the flowers, thus depleting the nectar supply for other pollinators.

This hummingbird was named after the fallen archangel Lucifer, who was also known as the bearer of light, the torchbearer, and the morning star. The genus name *Calothorax* is from the Greek *calo*, meaning "beautiful," and *thorax*, meaning "chest."

♀

Ruby-throated Hummingbird
Archilochus colubris

Spanish
Colibrí garganta de rubí, Chupaflor rubí, Mansoncito garganta
de fuego

Range: Southeastern Canada to Gulf states; winters mostly from
Mexico to western Panama; nests as far west as central Alberta
and central Texas.

The only hummingbird found regularly east of the Great Plains,
the ruby-throated hummingbird is also remarkable in its
migration pattern. Many individuals migrate nonstop across the
Gulf of Mexico—six hundred miles over open water—flying low
over the tops of waves. In preparation for this hazardous journey,
birds must double their body mass by fattening up on nectar and
insects prior to departure. Other individuals favor a more cautious
approach, choosing to fly over land and following the coastal
route around the Gulf of Mexico.

In addition to feeding on insects and floral nectar, the ruby-
throated hummingbird often feeds on tree sap provided by the
drilling of sapsuckers in more northerly locations. This species is
especially attracted to the blooms of trumpet creeper (*Campsis
radicans*), which seems to be primarily adapted to pollination by

♀

♂

these birds. Ruby-throated hummingbirds are also attracted to bee balm, columbine, and red salvia.

Both males and females have iridescent green backs. Undersides are grayish white, with dusky green sides and flanks. Closely related to the black-chinned hummingbird of more westerly states, the female ruby-throat is essentially identical in appearance to the female black-chin. When seen in the right light, male ruby-throats reveal fiery red gorgets. Both sexes produce humming sounds with their wings during flight. A rapid squeaky *chip* note is delivered during aggressive interactions. When not engaged in acts of aggression, their call is a soft *tew*.

Females spend six to ten days constructing their nests, lacing plant material together with spider webbing and using down from plants such as thistles and dandelions. The site is usually on a horizontal branch or one that slopes downward in a tree like maple, beech, or hemlock. Ruby-throated hummingbirds may also select large shrubs for nesting locations and often reuse old nests. After the eggs hatch, the chicks are blind at first and beg for food in response to air movement from the female's wings as she brings food to the nest.

Most individuals migrate to Mexico or farther south for the winter, but some individuals spend the winter in the southeastern U.S.

Black-chinned Hummingbird

Archilochus alexandri

Spanish
Colibrí Gorjinegro

Range: Summers from British
Columbia to central Texas and
southern California; winters in
Mexico.

♀

Widespread at low elevations in the West, black-chinned hummingbirds live in a variety of habitats from urban gardens to dry desert washes. Males and females are about three inches long and have metallic green backs. The male has a black chin or throat, bordered below by a patch of iridescent purple. Female and young black-chinned hummingbirds have pale gray or whitish underparts, dusky streaks on the throat, and white outer tail feathers. They are almost identical to the female and young ruby-throated hummingbirds of the east, which are close relatives.

In some parts of the west, black-chinned hummingbirds are important pollinators of beardtongue (*Penstemon barbatus*) and paintbrush (*Castilleja* spp.). They also feed on the flowers of other penstemons, agaves, chuparosa, delphinium, and desert honeysuckle, and are readily attracted to feeders filled with sugar water. Black-chinned hummingbirds may drink water when it is available, but obtain most of their liquid from the nectar they consume. At flowers or at feeders, they typically flip and spread their tails almost continuously. They rarely perch while feeding at flowers, but may do so at feeders.

Like other species, black-chinned hummingbirds cannot survive exclusively on a diet of nectar or sugar water. In order to obtain other dietary elements, they eat small insects and spiders, sometimes flying from a perch to capture a single specimen and then returning to the same spot. More frequently, they take multiple small insects in quick succession from a swarm. They also harvest small insects and spiders from the leaves of plants.

Male black-chinned hummingbirds perform a pendulum-like courtship display, flying back and forth in front of the female in wide, U-shaped arcs, and making whirring sounds on each pass. There is no apparent pair bond; the two sexes come together only for copulation, and females are responsible for all nest-building activities. The nest is a deep cup made of plant fibers and plant down, held together with spider silk. Females may reuse old nests, but this usually involves construction of a new one on top of the old. The female generally lays two white, unmarked eggs. After an incubation period of about two weeks, the female begins feeding the young a diet of regurgitated nectar and insects. The strong yet flexible nests stretch out to accommodate the growing nestlings.

The voice of the black-chinned hummingbird is nearly identical to that of ruby-throated hummingbird—a soft *tew* accompanied by incessant chattering.

♂

Anna's Hummingbird
Calypte anna

Spanish
Colibrí coronirrojo

Range: Very common, Pacific Coast north to British Columbia, east to Arizona.

♀

A familiar nesting bird of western gardens, Anna's hummingbird has expanded its range in two directions in recent years—north along the Pacific Coast and east into Arizona. The range expansion is probably due in part to the widespread use of plants that bloom all year long. This species feeds eagerly on the flowers of non-native plants, including blue gum, a type of eucalyptus planted extensively as a windbreak in some parts of the West. Blue gum flowers provide a ready supply of nectar in the winter months. Naturalized tree tobacco (*Nicotiana glauca*), a native of South America, blooms when natives do not and also provides nectar-rich flowers. Also, widespread use of sugar water feeders has undoubtedly contributed to the range expansion of this species.

Anna's are chunky-looking hummingbirds with bright metallic green backs and gray underparts. Males have rose-red crowns and throats. Females are more plain-looking, but they usually show a small patch of red on the throat, and tend to be more dingy gray underneath than other hummingbirds. More vocal than most other species, the male Anna's has a rather unmelodic song that is a series of repetitive scratchy notes, often delivered while perched.

For his courtship display, the male Anna's hovers in midair, delivering his buzzy song, then flies very high and plummets toward the female. At the end of the dive, he abruptly pulls up and makes a distinctive, loud popping noise. Some individuals begin nesting as early as December. Females build nests out of plant fibers and spider webs, and often use lichens to camouflage the outside of the structure. Western scrub-jays are regular nest predators that consume the tiny hummingbird eggs.

Anna's hummingbirds have an interesting migration route. Southwestern birds often migrate east to west. Many Arizona birds fly west to California in mid-spring and return in later summer.

Anna's was named for Anna de Belle Massena, the beautiful Princess of Rivoli who lived in the 1800s. Her husband, Francois Massena, the Duke of Rivoli, was the inspiration for the name of Rivoli's hummingbird, now called magnificent hummingbird. The genus name for Anna's, *Calypte*, means "hidden" in Greek, undoubtedly a reference to the elusiveness of the color on the bird's throat patch, or gorget.

Anna's hummingbirds are thought to be significant pollinators of currant, gooseberry (*Ribes* spp.), monkey flower (*Mimulus* spp.), and penstemon, particularly the genus *Keckiella*.

♂

Costa's Hummingbird

Calypte costae

Spanish
Colibrí Costa, Colibrí Coronivioleta Desértico, Chupamirto garganta

Range: Deserts of southwestern U.S. (mainly Arizona and California) and northwestern Mexico.

With its iridescent violet crown and flared violet gorget, the male Costa's hummingbird is a stunning sight. This small hummingbird often perches high on the dead twigs of acacia, palo verde, or ironwood trees where it scans for other hummingbirds—male or female—entering its territory. In order to attract a mate, the males perform daring aerial courtship displays. Rising high in the air, often one hundred feet or more, they plunge downward while making a shrill, continuous whistle. At the bottom of the dive, they pull up sharply and then fly upward again. This distinctive whistled vocalization is often what catches your attention. A dry *tic* describes the regular call note for both sexes. Females have green backs, are dingy white below, and their crowns are often a dull brown color.

Hot and dry areas west of the Continental Divide and south of the Great Basin are home to Costa's hummingbirds. In the California and Arizona deserts, numbers peak in March or April, but by May or June most of the birds leave the desert scrub to migrate to the Pacific Coast. Two

♀

important plants for these hummingbirds are ocotillo (*Fouquiera splendens*) and chuparosa (*Justicia californica*). Chuparosa is particularly reliable as a source of nectar because it may bloom well into the winter months. Opportunistic in seeking nectar sources, Costa's often probe into the tiny flowers of desert lavender (*Hyptis emoryi*) as well as the much larger white blooms of the saguaro cactus (*Carnegiea gigantea*).

Particularly well adapted to hot and dry climates, Costa's hummingbirds become less active and often retreat to shade on blistering hot days. Birds sometimes tighten and compress their feathers, adopting an upright cylindrical posture that helps to facilitate heat loss. They may also open their mouths with a panting-like behavior. As air flows in over the saliva in their mouths, it helps cool down the body, working in much the same manner as an evaporative cooler.

Costa's hummingbird was named for Louis Marie Panteleon Costa, a French nobleman of the early 1800s who was interested in many aspects of natural history, including birds. He was particularly fascinated with hummingbirds and owned an impressive selection of specimens.

Calliope Hummingbird
Stellula calliope

Spanish

Chupamirto rafaguitas, Colibrí gorgirrayado

Range: Summers in mountains of western North American from southwest Canada to Baja; winters in Mexico.

The calliope hummingbird, the smallest bird in North America, is predominately a species of the mountains. Despite its tiny size, it is able to survive cold summer nights at high elevations in the Rocky Mountains and Sierra Nevada. Calliope hummingbirds nest almost to timberline, 10,000-11,500 feet, and prefer edges of mountain meadows rimmed by conifers, or canyons and aspen thickets along mountain streams. The nest site is usually on a twig or branch under overhanging foliage, which helps provide some protection against the cold. Females sometimes build their nests on the base of an old pinecone, camouflaging their cuplike nests to look like part of the cone.

Calliope hummingbirds migrate in a northwesterly direction through the Pacific lowlands in early spring. Males generally arrive at the breeding grounds before the females. Beginning in July, they travel southeast through the mountains to their wintering grounds in Mexico.

♂

♀

Male calliope hummingbirds have a unique throat patch. The reddish purple on the throat forms streaks or rays, and birds sometimes elevate these feathers, producing a starburst display. Against the white background of the throat, the brightly streaked pattern is stunning. Males are green above and white below with greenish sides. Females and young birds—with their green backs, lightly spotted throats, and buffy undersides—are similar in appearance to young and female rufous and Allen's humming-birds, but are smaller and have relatively short bills and tails. The Calliope's call note is a high, thin *tsip*.

This species regularly perches on the tip of a willow or other shrub and flies out like a flycatcher to snap up flying insects. They also typically feed at sap wells, holes in trees created by woodpeckers known as sapsuckers. Like other high-elevation hummingbirds, they regularly hover at the flowers of paintbrush, scarlet gilia (*Ipomopsis aggregata*), and penstemon to garner nectar.

John Gould, a well-known English ornithologist of the 1800s, is responsible for naming calliope hummingbird. The Latin genus name *Stellula* means "little star" and refers to the starburst pattern created by the streaked gorget of the male.

Broad-tailed Hummingbird

Selasphorus platycercus

Spanish
*Colibrí Vibrador, Chupamirto
cola ancha*

Range: Breeds in south and
central Rockies and mountains of
the Great Basin south into western
Texas and Mexico; winters from
Mexico to Guatemala.

♂

This classic hummingbird of the mountain West frequents
high elevation meadows and forests to over 10,000 feet,
where it feeds on red tubular flowers such as penstemon, red
columbine, scarlet gilia (*Ipomopsis aggregata*), and betony. Males
of this species create distinctive, high-pitched trilling sounds
with certain wing feathers while flying. This wing trill may be
heard as the birds navigate over lowland areas during migration.

Wing trilling is part of the male's aggressive behavior in
defending his territory. Males often launch from willow thickets
in mountain meadows for their display flights. Courtship rituals
include a series of high climbs, dives, and hoverings accompanied
by the resonant wing trill. Males also make a repetitive chittering
call when intruding birds appear on the scene. Females may
chitter in contests over nesting and feeding sites, or as a means
of distracting enemies away from their nests.

Nest construction for the female broad-tailed hummingbird
begins when the food supply is adequate; that is, when nectar is
readily available. Nests are generally located on low horizontal
branches of willow, alder, pine, fir, spruce, or aspen trees, four
to fifteen feet from the ground. The nest is often sheltered from
above by an overhanging branch, which aids in heat conservation.
Females may take four to five days to build a new nest, although
less time is required if they choose to rebuild on material from a

previous year's nest. After collecting various plant materials, the female forms the cuplike nest by rotating her body and tamping her feet. She builds the lip of the nest by making side-to-side movements with her chin along the edge. Nests are usually anchored to branches with spider webbing.

Male and female broad-tailed hummingbirds have blue-green backs, and the males sport brilliant rosy-pink throats. Females and young birds are whitish underneath with some reddish brown on the flanks and at the sides of the tail.

In addition to red tubular flowers, broad-tailed hummingbirds also feed on atypical hummingbird flowers such as pussy willows. They also consume small gnats or flies from insect swarms and snatch aphids from grasses and other vegetation. Broad-tailed hummingbirds may use sap as a nectar substitute, and are often seen feeding at the sap wells created in willow bark by red-naped sapsuckers.

♀

Rufous Hummingbird
Selasphorus rufus

Spanish
Chupamirto dorado, Colibrí colica

Range: Pacific Northwest to south central Alaska; winters in Mexico; small numbers winter in Gulf Coast states.

One can always tell when a rufous hummingbird is in the vicinity. These particularly feisty birds—named for the male's overall rufous, or reddish brown, color—are very vocal and will aggressively drive away other birds that attempt to approach patches of flowers or feeders in their territory. They keep up an incessant buzzy chatter, and the wings of the male also produce a distinctive metallic whine in flight. While asserting his territorial prerogative, a male may also fan his tail, displaying its bright rufous coloration. Males also have brilliant reddish brown backs with flaming orange-red throats. Females and young birds are plainer in appearance but have rufous on both the tail and sides.

Rufous hummingbirds are champion long-distance migrants, wintering in Mexico and nesting as far north as southern Alaska— farther north than any other hummingbird. They migrate north-ward through the Pacific lowlands to take advantage of early flowering spring blossoms. In mid- to late summer, they return

♀

♂

south through the Rocky Mountains and Sierra Nevada, refueling on flowering plants such as scarlet gilia (*Ipomopsis aggregata*), penstemon, salvias, and paintbrush.

Courtship displays by males involve a steep "U" or vertical oval flight pattern, followed by a dive. Whining and popping sounds are delivered at the bottom of the dive. Rufous males also engage in a behavior known as whisking. As the female perches low in vegetation, the male performs a series of buzzing oscillations in three-dimensional figure eights, suggesting the motion of a whisk broom. Breeding grounds are usually forest edges and clearings, often along streams. Nests are generally well hidden in the lower part of a coniferous tree, deciduous shrub, or vine, three to thirty feet up.

Allen's Hummingbird

Selasphorus sasin

Spanish
Chupamirto petirrojo, Zumbador de Allen

Range: Nests from southwestern Oregon to southwestern California; winters in Mexico. Non-migratory race on the Channel Islands and Palos Verdes Peninsula in southern California.

♀

Allen's hummingbird is one of two common nesting hummingbirds found in northern California gardens. This species is a very early migrant. Males begin arriving at their breeding grounds as early as January, and are followed by the females. Many of these birds are headed south by the end of June.

In flight, males make a high-pitched, metallic buzzing sound with certain wing feathers. Their dive display is relatively complex. Swinging back and forth in pendulous arcs, males pause at the top of each arc to shake their bodies and emit a loud buzz. They then rise one hundred feet or so in the air before beginning an impressive power dive. While delivering a loud metallic shriek, they pull out of the dive just above the object of their display. This exhibition is usually part of the mating ritual, but also may be an act of aggression against other hummingbirds that may invade their territory. Males may strike intruders with their bills or feet following this display. Occasionally dive displays seem to have no apparent object whatsoever, and may be simply a way of advertising territory.

Female Allen's hummingbirds generally raise two broods. Nests are usually located in a tree or shrub on a horizontal or diagonal branch as high as ninety feet above ground. They sometimes nest in buildings. The thin outer nest layers are composed of bits of grass and leaves woven together with spider webs and decorated with lichens and moss. Females scrape spider webbing off their bills by means of a backward-forward flight while hovering over the nest. They then adjust the webbing with the tips of their bills. Downy plant material is used for the interior of the nest.

On the breeding grounds, bush monkeyflower (*Mimulus aurantiacus*), paintbrush (*Castilleja* spp.), columbine (*Aquilegia formosa*), and currants and gooseberries (*Ribes* spp.) are among their favorite nectar plants.

Males begin leaving the breeding grounds for their southward migration while females are still raising young. Then females depart, followed by the young birds. On the return trip to their wintering grounds, some individuals follow an inland route along the Sierra Nevada and coastal mountain ranges in order to take advantage of flowers blooming at higher elevations.

The genus name *Selasphorus* means "flame-bearing" and undoubtedly refers to the bright reddish orange throat of the male. Males also have metallic green backs, reddish brown sides, rump, tail, and cheeks. Females and young birds have reddish brown on their tail feathers and sides and are quite similar in appearance to female and young rufous hummingbirds. The two species are virtually indistinguishable in the field.

♂

The following hummingbird species are very rare visitors to the United States and are generally not found at all during an average year.

Green-breasted Mango
Anthracothorax prevostii

Spanish
Chupaflor Gorjinegro

This species is widespread in the American tropics around forests and clearings in tropical lowlands. It has wandered north to south Texas a few times, mainly during the fall months. Large and bulky, the males are dark with a purple tail. The throat is black bordered by emerald green, and the center of the belly is a deep blue-green. Females have white underparts with a broad dark stripe down the center. Green-breasted mangos have slightly curved bills.

Xantus's Hummingbird

Hylocharis xantusii

Spanish
Colibrí Peninsular

A specialty of the southern half of Baja California, this bird has been sighted in southern California and once in British Columbia. Males have green throats, red bills with black tips, and white stripes behind the eye. Underparts are mainly cinnamon colored, and the tails are chestnut. Females lack the green throat, but also have buff-colored underparts, black-tipped red bills, and white behind the eyes.

Cinnamon Hummingbird

Amazilia rutila

Spanish
Amazilia Canela

This colorful hummingbird is common in semi-open country and woodland edges in parts of western and southern Mexico. It was not recorded in the U.S. until 1992 when an individual was spotted in southern Arizona. Both males and females have green backs and bright cinnamon underparts. Tails are reddish brown, and bills are red tipped with black.

HUMMINGBIRD GARDENING

If you want to lure hummingbirds into your garden, you simply have to create suitable habitat for them. The number of individuals that may spend time in your yard is closely related to the availability of food, water, nesting sites, and places to perch—necessities for hummingbird survival. Planting the right types of flowering plants will go a long way toward attracting these spellbinding creatures.

Hummingbirds as Pollinators

Hummingbirds play an important role in nature because they are responsible for pollinating certain kinds of flowers. Flowering plants rely on insects, birds, and other animals to pick up pollen from the anther of one flower and deliver it to the stigma of another. Hummingbirds are particularly well suited for this role. As they flit among the flowers, feeding on nectar, they pick up grains of pollen on their foreheads, bills, and chins. The pollen is then carried to the flowers of other plants.

The plant and the pollinator have a mutualistic relationship and each derives an important benefit from the other. For the flower, the benefit is the transport and appropriate placement of pollen, which ensures the reproduction of the plant species. For the hummingbird, the reward is in the form of the flower's nectar, a food essential for its own survival.

Over millions of years, flowers have evolved particular shapes, colors, and enticing fragrances not to appeal to humans but rather to attract pollinators and ensure the plant's survival. Flowers that have evolved to be pollinated by hummingbirds usually have a slender, tubular shape and are often some shade of red or orange.

Long, tubular flowers generally have more nectar at the base, which is difficult for bees and other insects to reach. These types of flowers and the long bills and tongues of tiny hummingbirds are adapted for each other. Some hummingbird flowers point

Female black-chinned hummingbird competes with bee for nectar.

to the side or downward, making it difficult for bees, butterflies, and other insects to land on them. Hummingbirds, of course, have the advantage of being able to hover at these types of flowers.

Red-orange flowers often contain the most nectar because this color range is poorly perceived by most insects. The color red decreases the likelihood that insects will have depleted the nectar supply before the hummingbirds arrive at the flower. Flowers pollinated by insects may have fragrant aromas, but flowers pollinated by hummingbirds are more likely to signal them with color instead. Hummingbirds will visit blooms of other colors, such as yellow and purple, but they are most likely to stop at those with reddish hues.

Tips for the Garden

Once you understand that hummingbirds are attracted to slender, tubular-shaped flowers in the red/pink/orange range, choosing shrubs and perennials with these flower characteristics is relatively straightforward. If possible, plant masses of the same species so that they will be more visible to passing birds and provide larger quantities of nectar. Include some plants like thistle that provide fuzzy material for nest linings. Plant trees to provide jumping-off points for courtship displays as well as places to perch and nest. Bare tree limbs or dead limbs make great perching sites from which hummers can survey their territories. Large tree trunks furnish lichen, which hummers often use to camouflage their nests.

The ideal habitat will have variety—sun, partial sun, and shade—and these conditions will enable you to grow a wider variety of plants. Plants of different heights provide choices for feeding, perching, and resting. A wider variety of plants will also give female hummingbirds more choices in terms of nesting materials. If you are fortunate enough to live in any area where hummers are found year round, be sure to choose flowering plants that bloom at different seasons.

Keep your garden looking natural. Hummingbirds are more likely to visit if there is a plenty of vegetation in which they can feel safe. Too much pruning and tidiness can actually discourage the birds from visiting your yard.

A healthy garden will have different varieties of plants and flowers that attract many insects. Hummingbirds regularly consume small insects, which serve as an important source of protein. Rarely do insects cause permanent damage to your plants, and their numbers are held in check by wild birds. Herbicides and pesticides should not be used in the bird garden. The use of pesticides probably will not get rid of all the insects, but it may get rid of the birds. Use biological controls, such as *Bacillus thuringiensis* (also known as BT), if necessary.

Using Native Plants

You can't go wrong using native plants. They are already adapted to local soil and climatic conditions and are generally more resistant to pests and diseases. Native plants provide native pollinators with the food for which they are best adapted. Remember that native plants and different hummingbird species have a long history of association.

The availability of native plants is much improved these days, and it is no longer necessary to seek out specialty nurseries to find them. Many conventional commercial nurseries now stock quite a variety, and catalog sales are also available. Some of the more difficult-to-locate species may be only available from seed.

Good Choices for the Hummingbird Garden

The following plant species, arranged by family, are native to the western U.S. and are particularly attractive to hummingbirds. So that you can be sure to ask for the correct plant when you visit the nursery, botanical names are included. Common names may vary from place to place and are not as reliable as the botanical names. For each species, the native range and habitat where the plant grows naturally are provided, as well as an indication of the flower color. Many books on gardening with natives are now available. These can provide further information about cultivation, watering requirements, and bloom periods. Check with your local native plant society for other suggested readings, as well as the location of native plant nurseries in your area.

Acanthus Family – Acanthaceae

Flameflower, flame acanthus (*Anisacanthus quadrifidus* var. *wrightii*): southern and western Texas and northern Mexico, rich soil in thickets; orange to orange-red

Desert honeysuckle (*Anisacanthus thurberi*): southwestern New Mexico, Arizona, and northern Mexico; rocky canyons and sandy washes, 2,000-5,000 feet; yellow to orange

Desert honeysuckle (Anisacanthus quadrifidus *var*. wrightii)

Chuparosa (Justicia californica)

Chuparosa (*Justicia californica*): southern Arizona, southeastern California, northwestern Mexico, washes and rocky slopes, sea level to 2,500 feet; deep red

Red justicia (*Justicia candicans*): southern Arizona and northern Mexico, rocky canyons and sandy washes, 1,500-3,500 feet; red-orange

Agave Family – Agavaceae

Red yucca, (*Hesperaloe parviflora*): central and southwestern Texas and northern Mexico; prairies, rocky slopes, and mesquite groves; shrimp pink to dark salmon

Bignonia Family – Bignoniaceae

Yellow bells (*Tecoma stans* var. *angustata*): southeastern Arizona, southern New Mexico, west Texas, south into Mexico, Central and South America; rocky slopes, gravelly plains and arroyos, 2,000-5,000 feet; yellow

Desert willow (*Chilopsis linearis*): western Texas to southern Nevada, Arizona, southern California, and northern Mexico; dry washes, up to 4,000 feet; pink to lavender

Yellow bells (Tecoma stans *var.* angustata)

Yellow columbine
(Aquilegia chrysantha)

Crowfoot Family – Ranunculaceae

Red columbine, western columbine (*Aquilegia formosa*): Alaska to Baja California, damp areas in mountains; scarlet red or orange

Yellow columbine (*Aquilegia chrysantha*): southern Colorado to New Mexico, Arizona, and northern Mexico; rich moist soil, 3,000-11,000 feet; yellow

Barbey's larkspur (*Delphinium barbeyi*): Wyoming, Colorado, Utah, New Mexico and eastern Arizona, sub-alpine mountains; purple

Scarlet larkspur (*Delphinium cardinale*): California coastal mountains south of Monterey, California, to Baja California; scarlet

Nelson's larkspur (*Delphinium nelsoni*): South Dakota to Idaho, south to Colorado, northern Arizona and Nevada; 6,000-8,500 feet; purple

Evening-Primrose Family – Onagraceae

Hummingbird trumpet (*Zauschneria californica* subspecies *latifolia*): From Trinity County, California, along the west slopes of the Sierra Nevada, south to San Diego County, southern Arizona, and east to southwest New Mexico; dry slopes and ridges up to 10,000 feet; red-orange

Castilleja *spp.*

Figwort Family – Scrophulariaceae

Paintbrush (*Castilleja integra*): Colorado, western Texas, New Mexico, Arizona, and northern Mexico; dryish rocky slopes among oaks and pines, 4,500-1,000 feet; vermilion bracts

Desert paintbrush (*Castilleja chromosa*): from eastern Oregon to Wyoming and south to New Mexico and southern California; open sagebrush flats, 5,000-8,000 feet; orange bracts

Bush monkeyflower, sticky monkeyflower (*Mimulus aurantiacus*): throughout California; chaparral, rocky slopes, open forest, below 5,000 feet; usually orange

Castilleja *spp.*

Juvenile Anna's hummingbird at sticky monkey flower (Mimulus aurantiacus).

Scarlet monkeyflower, crimson monkeyflower (*Mimulus cardinalis*): Utah to Oregon south to northwestern Mexico; damp areas in mountains, 2,000-8,500 feet; red to red-orange with yellow in the throat

Rock penstemon, cutleaf penstemon (*Penstemon baccharifolius*): western Texas; limestone crevices, 1,100-4,400 feet; cherry-red

Scarlet bugler (*Penstemon barbatus*): southern Colorado and Utah to central highlands of Mexico; in coniferous or oak woodlands, 4,000-10,000 feet; red

Firecracker beardtongue (*Penstemon eatoni*): southwestern Colorado to central Arizona and California; rocky slopes, 2,000-7,000 feet; orange-red to scarlet

Parry penstemon (*Penstemon parryi*): southern Arizona and Sonora, Mexico; washes, desert slopes and canyons, 1,500-5,000 feet; pink

Pineleaf penstemon (*Penstemon pinifolius*): from southern Arizona and New Mexico into Mexico; outcroppings and steep slopes from 6,000-8,500 feet; red-orange

Superb penstemon (*Penstemon superbus*): New Mexico, southeastern Arizona, Chihuahua, Mexico; rocky canyons and along washes, 3,500-5,500 feet; pinkish red

Male broad-tailed hummingbird at Penstemon *spp.*

Scarlet bugler (Penstemon barbatus)

Gooseberry Family – Grossulariaceae

Flowering currant (*Ribes sanguineum*): Pacific Northwest, British Columbia, Canada, western mountains; damp or moist areas in foothills and forested mountain slopes, to about 6,000 feet; deep pink

Fuschia flowering currant (*Ribes speciosum*): Santa Clara County, California, to Baja California, Mexico; coastal-sage scrub, chaparral, below 1,600 feet; red

Autumn sage (Salvia greggii)

Madder family – Rubiaceae

Smooth bouvardia (*Bouvardia glaberrima*): Southern New Mexico and Arizona, dry shady slopes and canyons, 3,000-9,000 feet; red-orange

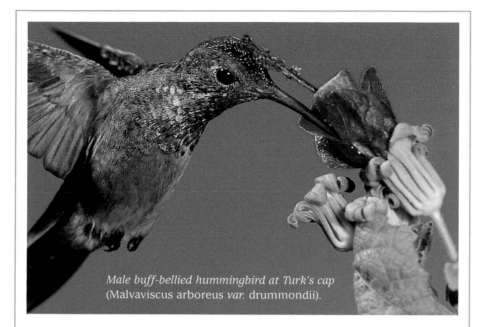

Male buff-bellied hummingbird at Turk's cap
(Malvaviscus arboreus *var.* drummondii).

Mallow Family – Malvaceae

Turk's cap, bleeding heart (*Malvaviscus arboreus* var. *drummondii*): Texas, Gulf Coast states to Mexico; roadsides, open sunny glades; red

Mint Family – Lamiaceae

Hummingbird mint, giant hyssop (*Agastache cana*): mountains of New Mexico and west Texas; 5,000-6,500 feet; rose pink

Tropical sage, scarlet sage (*Salvia coccinea*): South Carolina to east Texas and Mexico; woodlands and woodland edges; scarlet to crimson, occasionally pink

Autumn sage (*Salvia greggii*): Chihuahuan Desert region and south central Texas; canyons and rocky slopes, 2,200-5,800 feet; red-purple, orange-red to scarlet

Mountain sage (*Salvia regla*): west Texas and southward; rocky wooded slopes, pine-oak woodland; red to orange

Cleveland sage (*Salvia clevelandii*): San Diego County to Baja California; chaparral, coastal scrub in mountains mostly below 3,000 feet; blue to purple

Texas betony (Stachys coccinea)

Hummingbird sage, pitcher sage (*Salvia spathacea*): California, Solana County to Orange County; oak woodland, chaparral, coastal-sage scrub, open or shady slopes, below 2,800 feet; red

Cedar sage (*Salvia roemeriana*): Edwards Plateau and Trans-Pecos Texas; cedar breaks, oak woods, rocky areas in shade; scarlet

Texas betony, scarlet betony (*Stachys coccinea*): west Texas to southern Arizona and Mexico; canyons and slopes, 1,500-8,000 feet; vermilion

Bee balm (*Monarda menthifolia*): Canada to New Mexico and Arizona; mostly in pine forest; light purple

Morning glory Family – Convolvulaceae

Scarlet creeper, red morning glory (*Ipomoea coccinea*): west Texas to Arizona and south into tropical America, 2,500-6,000 feet; red

Ocotillo Family – Fouquieraceae

Ocotillo (*Fouquiera splendens*): west Texas to southeastern California and northern Mexico, rocky hillsides below 5,000 feet; bright red-orange

Pea Family – Fabaceae

Southwestern coral bean (*Erythrina flabelliformis*): southwestern New Mexico, southern Arizona, and northern Mexico; rocky canyons and hillsides, 3,000-5,000 feet; brilliant red

Fairy duster (*Calliandra eriophylla*): southwestern U.S. and Mexico; sandy washes, dry gravelly slopes and mesas, 1,000-5,000 feet; white to deep pink

Fairy duster (Calliandra eriophylla)

Phlox Family – Polemoniaceae

Skyrocket, scarlet gilia (*Ipomopsis aggregata*): Montana to British Columbia, south to New Mexico, Arizona, and California; 5,000-8,500 feet, mostly in open coniferous forests; bright red, sometimes pink or white

Pink Family – Caryophyllaceae

California Indian pink (*Silene californica*): California and southern Oregon; chaparral, oak woodland, coniferous forest, below 7,000 feet; vermilion

Mexican campion (Silene laciniata)

Mexican campion, Indian pink (*Silene laciniata*): western Texas to California and Mexico; mostly in pine forests, 5,500-9,000 feet; orange red

Saxifrage Family – Saxifragaceae

Coral bells (*Heuchera sanguinea*): Arizona and northern Mexico; damp rocky areas, 4,000-8,500 feet; pink to red

HUMMINGBIRD FEEDERS

Even though you may have planted a flowering feast in your garden, it never hurts to put up a sugar water feeder, which is guaranteed to attract hummingbirds. Hummer feeders come in a variety of shapes and sizes. The most important consideration in selecting one is its durability and ease of cleaning.

The standard recipe for hummingbird food is one part sugar to four parts water. Take a cup of granulated white table sugar and mix it with four cups of water. Boil for a few minutes to get out any impurities. Let it cool and then fill the feeder. Any unused portion can be refrigerated for later use. Red dye is not necessary; it's a foreign substance that wild birds can do without. Most hummer feeders have some sort of red on them, which is sufficient to attract the birds.

Cleanliness is of the utmost importance. In hot areas, sugar water solutions ferment quickly. Only fill the feeder with as much as you think the birds will drink in a day. Clean at least once a week, and more often in very hot weather.

Appropriately sized brushes and sponges for use in cleaning out feeders are now readily available at nature and wild bird stores. Baby bottle brushes also work. If the feeder becomes really moldy, you might consider using a very diluted solution of one part vinegar to five parts water. Some people also use a diluted bleach solution (one part bleach to 10 parts water). Just remember to rinse the feeder thoroughly after using vinegar or bleach solutions. If you are a purist and don't want to use any foreign material to clean your feeder, simply scrub with lots of hot water.

Never use honey as a sugar substitute. It may develop a fungus that affects the birds' tongues. Some prepackaged hummingbird food found at grocery stores often contains sodium benzoate as a preservative. Foreign substances like these are not natural, and probably not healthy for wild creatures.

If you have problems with bees or wasps, devices called bee guards fit over the feeding ports. However, these are not particularly effective, in part because they are often yellow, a color which is particularly attractive to bees. If swarms mob your feeder, take it down until the bees relocate elsewhere. In the meantime, hummingbirds can feed on your flowering plants.

Ant barriers are small receptacles filled with water that are placed on the hanging portion of the feeder. Ants, who always like a good sugar fix, cannot proceed beyond the water reservoir and thus cannot reach the sugar water.

If you live in a relatively mild climate and have hummingbirds year round, it is desirable to leave your sugar water feeders up all year. If you live in a cold climate, there is no point because there will be no hummingbirds present during the winter months. One myth that has been perpetuated over the years is that if you live in a cold area and leave your feeder up, it will prevent the birds from migrating. Like other birds, a hummingbird's instinct to migrate is deeply ingrained and the presence or absence of a feeder is unlikely to have any effect whatsoever. Occasionally a sick or weakened individual may stay at the feeder well into the fall because it is not up to the rigors of migration.

Male rufous hummingbird at feeder.

INDEX

ADDITIONAL READING

Kaufman, Kenn. *Lives of North American Birds.* Boston: Houghton Mifflin Co., 1996.

Lazaroff, David Wentworth. *The Secret Lives of Hummingbirds.* Tucson: Arizona-Sonora Desert Museum Press, 1995.

Newfield, Nancy L. and Nielsen, Barbara. *Hummingbird Gardens.* Shelburne, Vermont: Chapters Publishing Ltd., 1996.

Sayre, Jeff and April. *Hummingbirds—The Sun Catchers.* Minnetonka, Minnesota: Northword Press, 1996.

Stokes, Donald and Lillian. *The Hummingbird Book.* Boston: Little Brown and Co., 1989.

Toops, Connie. *Hummingbirds—Jewels in Flight.* Stillwater, Minnesota: Voyageur Press, 1992.